STREETS
PARKS
& LANES

OF COLLINGWOOD

ABBOTSFORD
CLIFTON HILL
& COLLINGWOOD

KAREN T CUMMINGS

COLLINGWOOD HISTORICAL SOCIETY, INC

2021

CONTENTS

Researched and written by Karen T Cummings with the assistance of other members of the Collingwood Historical Society.

Published 2021 by Collingwood Historical Society, Inc
PO Box 304 Clifton Hill 3068
www.collingwoodhs.org.au
ABN: 73 326 462 277
Registered No. A0030731L

ISBN: 978-0-6452041-6-2

FOREWORD

This publication updates and expands a previous publication by the Collingwood Historical Society, Streets of Collingwood (1991). This edition incorporates more streets and parks as well as considerable additional information which has since come to light.

The streets and parks have now been divided alphabetically into three sequences (Abbotsford, Clifton Hill and Collingwood). If you are searching for a particular street name but are unsure which section the street falls into, you can use the PDF search facility to find it.

ILLUSTRATIONS

Most photographs, plans and maps are courtesy of the State Library of Victoria. Details can be found in the Sources section at the end of the document.

Postcards of Smith and Johnston Streets ca 1906 to ca 1908

INTRODUCTION

How often do you stop to think about how your street got its name, or why it starts and ends where it does? The former City of Collingwood (incorporating Abbotsford, Clifton Hill and Collingwood) has its history written in its streets and the more one discovers about its past, the more meaningful the names and layout of the streets become.

At the end of 1838, only three years after the first European colonisation of Melbourne, the land which was to form much of the City of Collingwood was subdivided into portions to be sold by government auction in 1838–39. The area was not originally envisaged as urban: portions were around 25 acres each. The only reserves kept for roads were those on the boundaries, that is, the streets now known as Victoria Street, Smith Street, and Alexandra Parade, and also Johnston, Hoddle and Church Streets.

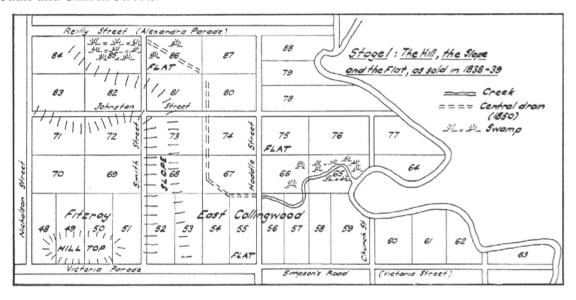

This illustration from Bernard Barrett's *The inner suburbs* shows the original portions prior to any further subdivision.

The purchasers were:

52 & 53 Stuart A Donaldson	54 & 55 JD Lyon Campbell	56 Hughes and Hosking
57 Charles Nicholson	58 William Bradley	59 Charles Nicholson
60 Stuart A Donaldson	61 W Lonsdale	62 John Thomas E Flint
63 William Richardson	64 Henry Smyth	65 & 66 Dieter L Campbell
67 JD Lyon Campbell	68 Stuart A Donaldson	73 George Otter
74 David Chambers	75 John Terry Hughes and John Hosking	
76 Charles James Garrard	77 Henry Smyth (May 1839)	78 Ranulph Dacre
79 JDL Campbell	80 & 81 John Terry Hughes and John Hosking	
86 James Stewart Ryrie	87 Archibald Mosman	88 John Dight

It was not long before some landowners began subdividing their landholdings or selling them on to others who did so. Until 1855, the main roads were the responsibility of Victoria's Central Roads Board while any minor roads were the responsibility of residents. The further development of streets did not proceed in a planned or orderly fashion. Looking at the illustration of the original portions, and the list of different owners, it becomes obvious why much of Collingwood ended up composed of short streets, provided by landholders when they subdivided their own piece of land, with no regard for overall design within the suburb. Subdividers were interested in profits and so usually tried to fit the maximum number of plots onto their parcel of land, without reference to what might be done on the next subdivision.

The 1850s were a boom time for subdivisions as Victoria's population swelled in response to gold fever. This illustration from Barrett's *The inner suburbs* shows the status of subdivisions in the early 1850s.

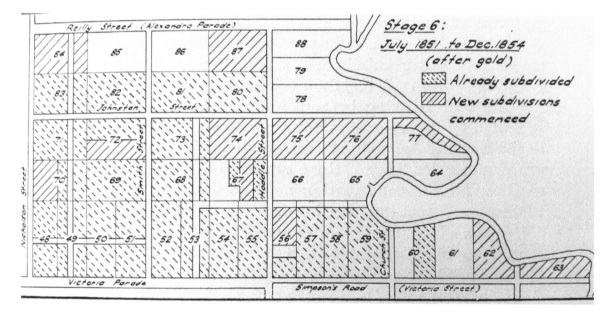

East Collingwood was proclaimed a municipality in 1855. Clement Hodgkinson, District Surveyor, later Surveyor-General of Victoria, was appointed Honorary Surveyor for the municipality and undertook a number of surveys. The Office of the Commissioner of Crown Lands and Survey issued, on 27 April 1857, **a list of 97 streets** which fixed the breadth of the carriage and foot ways of the said streets. A map indicating streets and buildings as of 1 January 1858 was eventually published (link below).

The new Council was faced with the problem of streets which did not meet up and over time had to buy up properties in order to rationalise street alignments. Some streets were also hampered in their development by the poor drainage of many parts of the Collingwood flat, indicated rather charmingly on Barrett's first sketch map by reedy marsh plants. As early as 1856 it was proposed at a Collingwood Council meeting that an Improvements Committee be appointed to report on the best means of extending the existing lines of streets and the formation of new ones for opening up direct communications. This problem remained a continuing topic of discussion at council meetings for decades and progress was usually slow. Gipps, Langridge and Wellington Streets are examples of thoroughfares that attained their final design only after many years of discussion and argument, dissension usually springing from the fact that most councillors were businessmen eager to see major traffic routes running past their business premises. In fact, streets were constantly discussed at council meetings: their kerbing, channelling, metalling, cleansing, draining, lighting, raising, lowering, and the wandering of animals thereon were the subject of a never-ending stream of correspondence from residents.

In 1873 the Town Clerk issued a notice that 'all streets, lanes and rights of way laid out through private property must be properly constructed by the owners of the property abutting thereon to the satisfaction of the Council, before streets can be proclaimed public streets or taken under the management of the council.'

With the 97 named streets inherited by the municipality of East Collingwood in 1855, most of the streets in the area south of Alexandra Parade were already in existence. One major exception was the large area around Victoria Park known as Dight's Paddock where subdivision did not begin until 1878. Much of east Clifton Hill was not subdivided until the 1880s and 1890s. Later changes to street lay-outs have been brought about by the railway line extension from Victoria Park to the city in 1901, the construction of large factories and Housing Commission flats, the widening of Hoddle Street and the freeway construction. Of course, a walk around Collingwood streets today will show that the layout of most streets never was rationalised; many run for only one or two blocks.

In the late twentieth century and the twenty-first century another round of changes has been taking place with very extensive building development. Many back lanes are now the site of residences and so need to be named, while further subdivisions have taken place on previously unused land. Schools and factories are being converted to flats and offices, leading to numbering changes or additional streets.

Foy & Gibson emporium in Smith Street and their factories in Oxford and Cambridge Streets, 1922

MAPS

The **Maps Online** page of the Collingwood Historical Society's website has links to a number of maps of Collingwood, which will help you follow the development of streets more easily. Of particular interest is Hodgkinson's map which shows all buildings as well as streets.

- Kearney, *Melbourne and its suburbs*, 1855?

- Hodgkinson, *Plan shewing the streets and buildings in existence in East Collingwood on January 1st 1858*

- H G De Gruchy & Co's new borough map, Melbourne district, 1869?

- Woodhouse, *City of Collingwood*, 1885

- *Municipality of Collingwood*, 1921?

- *City of Collingwood*, 1980s

Among other maps of interest which can be viewed on the State Library website are:

- Frederick Proeschel, Map of Collingwood, 1855?
  http://search.slv.vic.gov.au/permalink/f/1o9hq1f/SLV_VOYAGER968088

- Allotments in the City of Collingwood and Borough of Fitzroy, 1864
  http://search.slv.vic.gov.au/permalink/f/1tla8hv/SLV_VOYAGER2135611

- H. Byron Moore, *Plan of Melbourne and its suburbs*, 1879
  http://search.slv.vic.gov.au/permalink/f/1o9hq1f/SLV_VOYAGER787662

- New plan of Melbourne & suburbs, Sands & McDougall, 1873
  http://search.slv.vic.gov.au/permalink/f/1tla8hv/SLV_VOYAGER797182

> **You will find it useful to have the relevant maps open on your screen while reading about a particular period of development.**

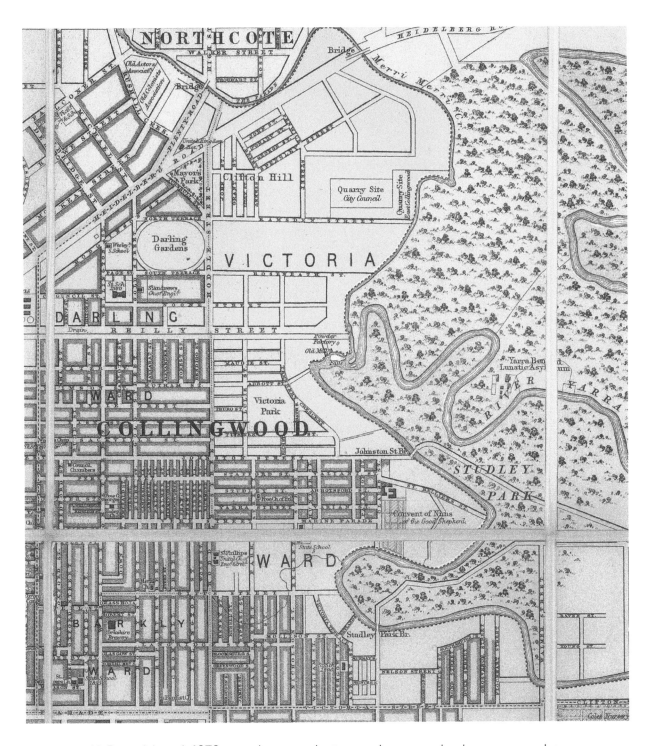

H. Byron Moore's 1879 map shows much nineteenth-century development complete, except for parts of Clifton Hill and Abbotsford.

NAMES

In the early period (and some later periods) subdividers chose the names of the streets and often commemorated themselves or their relatives, or chose names relating to important events, personages or places in Great Britain.

Later, it was common for streets to be named after councillors, a practice most recently carried out in the 1970s (McCutcheon Way). In some cases, street names were changed in order to provide a memorial for a councillor, or councillors were honoured in the naming of a park or reserve. Some streets derived their names from the large riverside estates which were gradually broken up.

Nowadays, naming or renaming roads, features, or localities follows the City of Yarra Place Naming Policy which operates under the Local Government Act 1989 and the Geographic Place Names Act 1998 in accordance with the Naming rules for places in Victoria, statutory requirements for naming roads, features and localities 2016. Council does not normally consider naming unless there is a property actually fronting the street to be named. Among the name forms excluded by the regulations are first names, or the name of a living person. The detailed policy can be found on this page:

https://www.yarracity.vic.gov.au/about-us/governance/place-naming

On council's website you can also find:

- Register of Public Roads (including laneways):
  https://www.yarracity.vic.gov.au/services/roads-and-traffic

- The origin of some street names (those included in the street signage project):
  https://www.yarracity.vic.gov.au/services/roads-and-traffic/street-signs-heritage

It is not always easy to find out after whom or what a street was named so in some cases we have relied on intelligent guesswork, as indicated in the text, and in other cases we simply do not know. Dating can also be problematic as streets are sometimes shown on plans before they exist physically, and years before building blocks and houses appear. Any further information will be gratefully received.

1880s councillors immortalised not only on the town hall foundation stone but also in street names (except for W Smith)

ABBOTSFORD

The area along the river was chosen largely by people who wanted to retain a large landholding in the semi-rural retreat of the 1840s, although it was not long before industrialists were also making use of the river for water supply and drainage. Landholdings closer to transport routes such as Victoria, Hoddle and Johnston streets were subdivided earlier, but gradually the large river-side properties were broken up, the largest being the 1880s development of Dight's Paddock which extended between Johnston, Hoddle and Alexandra Parade east and was the site of two 1840s houses, Dight's *Yarra House* and JDL Campbell's *Campbellfield*. Other riverside mansions also remained into the twentieth century with reduced landholdings. The name is derived from *Abbotsford House* which is believed to have been named after Sir Walter Scott's house In Scotland.

ABBOTT GROVE, ABBOTSFORD Originally the westerly end of Abbot Street, which was cut in two when the railway line was constructed.

ABBOTT STREET Part of the 1878 subdivision of Dight's Paddock, this was named after David Abbott, the solicitor who negotiated the purchase of Dight's Paddock from the Dight family on behalf of Edwin Trenerry in 1878 and organised the subdivision of 'The Campbellfield Estate'. The first auction was held in February 1878; council bought ten acres which was to become Victoria Park, so fresh plans were drawn up for a November auction. Sales continued over the next year or two until, after Trenerry died in April 1880, an auction was held 15 September 1880 for all remaining blocks, including Yarra House. The complete holding was bought by Mr J J Kelly. In October and November 1881 he began

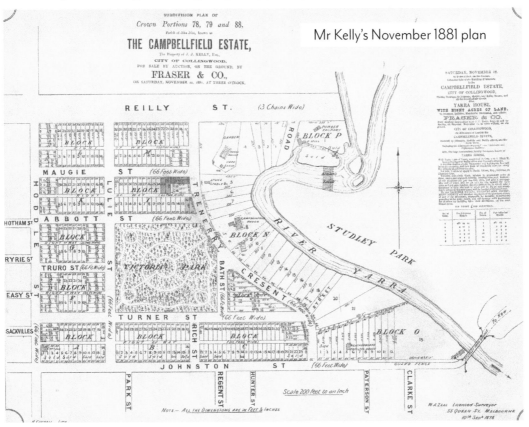

Mr Kelly's November 1881 plan

to auction these individually and auctions continued until December 1885. In 1887 there were still many vacant blocks of land in the Campbellfield Estate and even by 1900 they were not uncommon.

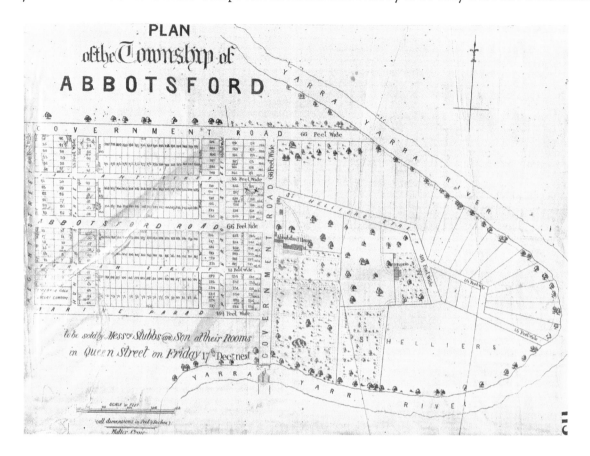

ABBOTSFORD STREET 1852. When John Orr of *Abbotsford House* began subdividing his extensive surrounding landholding, it was referred to as the new township of Abbotsford. This name was eventually adopted for the eastern portion of Collingwood. Sales of vacant blocks continued into the late 1850s.

ACACIA PLACE A street added when the former Honeywell site at the river end of Victoria Street was re-developed as Eden on the River around 2013. This is a private road.

ALBERT STREET 1855 or earlier. Possibly named after Queen Victoria's husband Albert, Prince of Saxe-Coburg and Gotha.

ALLAN STREET See Bloomburg Street

BATH STREET Part of Edwin Trenerry's 1878 subdivision of Dight's paddock. Named after Thomas Bath, an associate of Trenerry's in Ballarat and who like Trenerry came from the Parish of St Clement, near Truro in Cornwall. In 1853 Bath commenced business as a hotelkeeper in Lydiard street, Ballarat, at the premises now known as Craig's Royal Hotel. Sales of blocks in the subdivision continued over several years and Bath Street was first built on in the 1880s.

BLOOMBURG STREET Called Allan Street on Hodgkinson's 1858 map and the subdivision map below, but referred to as Bloomburg in council's 1857 list of streets.

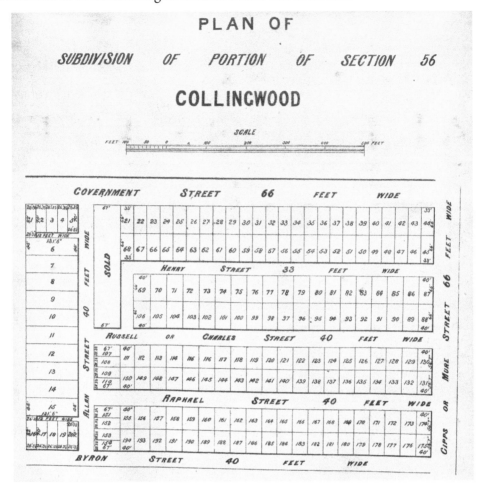

Plan of subdivision of portion of Section 56, indicating early vagaries of nomenclature

BOND STREET 1858. Several names in this subdivision derive from Mayfair (London) streets.

BRICK LANE See Flockhart Street

BROOK STREET The section of Southampton Crescent between Grosvenor Street and Duke Street was called Brook Street in the nineteenth century.

BENT STREET This street is now lost under the massive C.U.B. complex. The area was previously the riverside site of the mansion and garden of the wool-dealer Jesse Fairchild. In 1885 it was bought up by a syndicate headed by Thomas Bent, M.L.A. and sub-divided into 150 building allotments, although Fairchild's house was not demolished until the twentieth century.

BROWN RESERVE A small park in Nicholson Street which has existed since the early twentieth century.

BYRON STREET See Park Street

CHARLES STREET The section from Victoria Street to Gipps Street is shown on an 1855 map, but it was not extended through to Vere Street until the late 1880s. Perhaps named after Charles Nicholson, the early landowner of this area, whose property was first auctioned on 22 April 1851.

CHURCH STREET 1850s or earlier, a continuation of Church Street Richmond which dates from the 1840s. A bridge crossing the Yarra to Studley Park was constructed here in 1857 and demolished in 1902.

CLARKE STREET On an 1858 map this is called Government Road although by then Clarke was included on the list of streets in East Collingwood. The name probably refers to Captain Andrew Clarke, who in 1853 replaced Robert Hoddle as surveyor-general and was elected M.L.A. He was a prominent Freemason and officiated at the laying of the foundation stone of the nearby Johnston Street Bridge in 1856.

CLIFTON STREET the easternmost section of Victoria Street, between Walmer Street and the river, was named as Clifton Street on de Gruchy's ca 1869 map and Byron Moore's 1879 map, but was rationalised after the construction of the Victoria Street bridge in the 1880s.

COLLINS FOOTBRIDGE This gateway to the Yarra Bend Park that crosses the Yarra at the end of Gipps Street was probably named in honour of A. Collins, the mayor of Collingwood in 1912–13 around the time the bridge was built.

COOK STREET Part of the 1885 subdivision of Jesse Fairchild's property, it commemorates the maiden surname of Jesse Fairchild's mother.

DIGHTS FALLS Off Trenerry Crescent, this tranquil area of natural beauty includes some remains of **John Dight's** flour mill which was powered by the falls.

DUKE STREET A street in an 1858 subdivision, its name is assumed to refer to the London street.

EDDY COURT Randolph 'Dolph' Eddy was a Collingwood councillor in the 1960s and 1970s and also became a state parliamentarian.

FAIRCHILD STREET Jesse Fairchild, a wool merchant, owned a mansion and large garden in the area now dominated by Carlton & United Breweries. This street was created when the property was subdivided into 138 building allotments in the 1880s. Fairchild's house remained in a reduced but still substantial garden setting fronting the newly created Fairchild Street.

FEDERATION LANE This was an unnamed right-of-way for many years, until the construction of town houses

on the site of the Victoria Park school necessitated naming for the address of the residences facing the rear.

FERGUSON STREET 1855 or earlier. Shown, probably in error, on Hodgkinson's 1858 map as Regent Street, which is the name of the street on the Richmond side of Victoria Street, directly opposite (not to be confused with the Regent street which became Nicholson Street).

FLOCKHART STREET Robert Flockhart, a tanner, was a councillor from 1861 to 1864. This street was originally called Brick Lane and was the centre of the numerous brickworks that flourished in the area from the 1850s to the 1890s. There were also Chinese market gardens on both sides of the street. Nowadays, at the end of the street in a picturesque space on the banks of the Yarra, is FLOCKHART RESERVE.

GAHAN RESERVE John Gahan, born in England in 1851, came to Abbotsford in 1856. He was a very active member of the congregation at St. Philip's Church of England in Hoddle Street, being secretary of the Sunday School for 16 years. He ran a contracting business in Victoria Street and was a councillor from 1887 until 1911, serving three terms as Mayor, in 1893-94 and 1902-04. The reserve was named in 1906 or 1907. Among other things Gahan was an advocate of public baths for Collingwood.

GIPPS STREET, Abbotsford See Collingwood.

GREENWOOD STREET Thomas Greenwood was a councillor from 1856 until 1865 (including a term as Mayor in 1863-4) and again in 1868-69.

GROSVENOR STREET This was named after one of the early riverside properties *Grosvenor Lodge*, part of which was subdivided in 1858 by **Eardley Blois Norton**, who had been farming on the property. The auction on January 25th, 1859 also included land in South Audley, Bond and Duke Streets (all streets in close proximity to Grosvenor Street in Mayfair) and Southampton Crescent, the whole being described as the Grosvenor Estate.

HARPER STREET This street was not created until the late 1920s and was always a location for industrial and commercial buildings. The part of Abbotsford between Marine Parade, Gipps Street, Nicholson Street and the Yarra River remained undeveloped later than surrounding areas because the Blind Creek and associated drainage meandered through the area to the Yarra. A sepia wash and ink sketch of 1854 depicts the creek entering the Yarra.

G B Richardson, Creek and Old Watering Stage, on the Yarra, East Collingwood, 1854

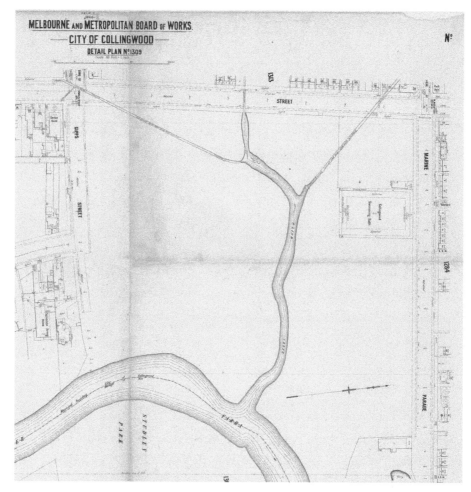

MMBW Detail Plan showing the Blind Creek in 1901

HENRY STREET The existing Henry Street dates from prior 1857. Some older maps also name Yarra Street between Hoddle and Nicholson Street as Henry Street. See also Henry Street Collingwood.

HODDLE STREET See Collingwood

HUNTER STREET Part of John Orr's 1852 subdivision called the Township of Abbotsford.

JAMES STREET 1850s, originally called St James Street, perhaps a reference to the street and district of that name in London.

JOHNSTON STREET See Collingwood

KELLY STREET A small street created between Fairchild and Cooke Streets in the area developed in the late 1880s as part the subdivision of the Jesse Fairchild estate (see Fairchild Street) but later covered by the C.U.B. complex. A probable source of the name is Hugh Kelly, a Langridge Street publican who was elected to council in 1881, helped to bring about the extension of Langridge Street through to Gertrude Street in 1882, and features on the Town Hall foundation stone.

LANGRIDGE STREET See Collingwood

LITHGOW STREET Part of an area subdivided in 1851. It possibly refers to William Lithgow who was Auditor-General for New South Wales from 1824 to 30 April 1852.

LITTLE CHARLES STREET While having the appearance of a lane, especially the section between Langridge St and Victoria St, this was quite a populous street in the 1880s although only a few of the old houses remain. A number of units have been constructed here towards the end of the twentieth century and in the twenty-first century.

LITTLE NICHOLSON STREET Half a dozen people were listed in the Sands and McDougall Directory as living in this right of way in the 1890s, while the council rate books referred to them as either 'off' William Street, 'off' Nicholson Street, or 'off' Mollison Street. Such houses were often built in the back yard of another house. One of those old houses remains, facing Little Nicholson Street, but accessed by a gate and path next to 23, its address now 23A William Street. More recently a new house has been built with the address 14 Little Nicholson Street.

LIVERPOOL STREET 1858 or earlier, presumably named after the city in England. The short street which ran from Gipps Street to Vere Street disappeared in 1900 to make way for the railway line extension.

LULIE STREET Part of Edwin Trenerry's subdivision of Dight's Paddock. Trenerry had just married Louisa Rich; Lulie was a diminutive form of Louisa.

MARINE PARADE Part of John Orr's 1852 subdivision (see Abbotsford Street) of 'The new township of Abbotsford'. This was one of the broader streets in the subdivision, but its name is rather puzzling given its distance from the sea. Lots for sale were referred to as 'fronting the Yarra'.

MASON'S LANE A narrow lane between 339 and 341 Johnston Street.

MAUGIE PLACE, MAUGIE STREET This unusual name in Edwin Trenerry's 1878 subdivision must have had some relevance for him but the source cannot be established with certainty. A possibility is a William Maughan, who was mining in the Ballarat district at the same time as Trenerry. Marked on Byron Moore's 1879 map, although subdivision into the present-day building blocks had not yet been completed. On J J Kelly's 1881 auction plan, Maugie Place is an unnamed right of way, but by 1904 further subdivision of the eight lots at the Trenerry Crescent end had taken place. Maugie Place and the houses on the north side of Maugie Street made way for the freeway in the 1970s.

MAY STREET This street no longer exists. Along with its neighbour River Terrace, it was prone to flooding in the years when the Yarra was badly flooded, such as 1891 and 1934. After 1934 May Street disappeared and Yarra Falls Ltd took over the land. In the 1990s the bluestone edging showing where May Street ran off the south side of Turner Street could still be seen, but this was removed when the housing development in Turner Street was constructed.

MAYFIELD STREET *Mayfield* was the home of <u>**Georgiana McCrae**</u>, the watercolourist and diarist known for her descriptions of life in Melbourne in the 1840s. The property was on nine acres, the house itself being located in the area now bounded by Church, Murray, and Mayfield Streets. Abbotsford was a rural area at the time that she and her husband lived at Mayfield, and she refers to her nearest neighbours as the Currs and Orrs (who lived in the area later occupied by the Convent of the Good Shepherd). The house was later owned by <u>**Sir Francis Murphy**</u>, Speaker in the House, and was finally demolished in 1962 although subdivision of the land had taken place some time earlier. Mayfield Street seems to date from the late 1880s.

MOLLISON STREET Part of an 1850s subdivision. Garryowen refers to Mollison as a landowner, and a William Mollison was elected to the Legislative Council in 1853. If this is the man after whom the street was named, nearby William Street may also refer to him.

MURRAY STREET On 1855 map.

NELSON STREET 1857 or earlier, but not extensively built on until after the subdivision of Jesse Fairchild's property in 1885. Prior to this it gave access to the large riverside properties of Frederick Row and **Richard Goldsbrough**.

NICHOLSON STREET Charles Nicholson, a Sydney resident, was a pastoralist and large landowner. His subdivision of the area bounded by Church, Victoria and Gipps Streets was first advertised in April 1851 and dealings continued until 1870. Blocks were advertised as an opportunity for recent immigrants to become freeholders. The plan at right is probably the one prepared for the auction sale 11 May 1859. Nicholson Street at first began at Victoria Street and finished at Gipps Street while another street called Regent Street ran from Johnston Street to Vere Street. Eventually Regent Street was extended to Gipps Street, yet again involving council in purchasing private properties, although the area between Vere Street and Gipps Street was largely undeveloped until the mid 1880s due to drainage problems. In November 1884 council resolved to rename Regent Street Nicholson Street, and the construction of the Town Hall in 1885 to 1887 encouraged more settlement in the area.

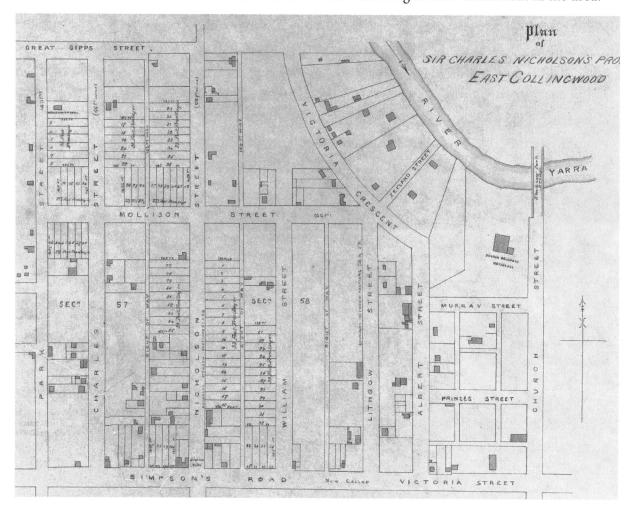

PARK STREET 1855 or earlier. Gahan Reserve did not exist then, so it was not the source of the name. Park Street from Victoria Street to Gipps Street was at first called Byron Street. Note that the two sections of the street developed separately and are not aligned.

PATERSON STREET 1855 or earlier.

PETERS LANE Once an unnamed back lane between Yarra Street and Studley Street

PRINCES STREET 1855 or earlier, perhaps part of Charles Nicholson's 1851 subdivision. A London street.

RAPHAEL STREET On the 1857 list of East Collingwood streets.

REGENT STREET A London street. See Nicholson Street and Ferguson Street, both of which previously had the name Regent.

RICH STREET This was part of Edwin Trenerry's subdivision of Dight's Paddock in 1878; he had just married Louisa Rich.

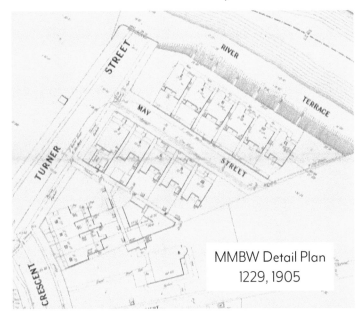

MMBW Detail Plan 1229, 1905

RIVER TERRACE This used to run very close to the river off Turner Street and was prone to severe flooding. After the major flood of 1934, both River Terrace and May Street disappeared; Yarra Falls Ltd took over the land and built the still-existing concrete flood wall. See the notes from the **2019 Collingwood History Walk** for more details.

River Terrace and May Street 1901

RUSSELL STREET 1850s. Perhaps named after the London street. Residents complained to Council about the state of its footpath in 1873.

SHAMROCK STREET The Shamrock Brewery was located in Victoria Street and this street seems to have been created to provide the brewery site with rear access from Flockhart Street.

SIMPSON'S ROAD See Victoria Street

SOUTH AUDLEY STREET 1858. Apparently named after a London street in company with several surrounding streets.

SOUTHAMPTON CRESCENT Part of the Grosvenor Estate (see plan below, to be auctioned by Symons & Perry), which was subdivided from 1858, and apparently named after the London street. See also Brook Street.

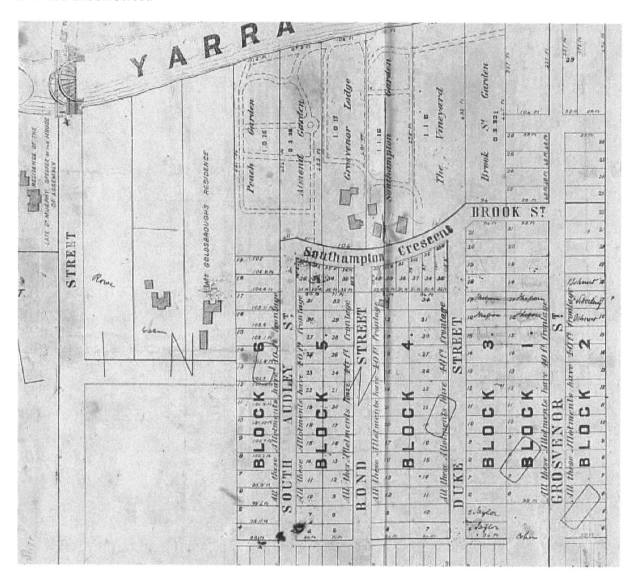

ST. HELIER'S STREET One of the early riverside houses built along the Yarra in the 1840s was that of **Edward Curr**. It was called St. Heliers (or Helier's) and gave its name to the street at the end of which it was located. (The road reservation continues to the river although the existing street stops well short of it). Curr's house was demolished in 1877. A later house in the street was also called St. Helier's. This was located closer to Clarke Street and was the residence of Sir Arthur Snowden who was elected to the Collingwood Council in 1868. His support for the Yarra anti-pollution laws led to violent clashes with other councillors and he remained on council for only one year but was later Lord Mayor of Melbourne from 1892 to 1895.

ST. JAMES STREET See James Street.

ST. PHILIP'S STREET Dates from the late 1880s. This area was not settled until later than the surrounding parts of Abbotsford because of drainage problems. The building of the Town Hall in 1886–7 gave an impetus to the area. Presumably it was named after St. Philip's Church of England which had been built in Hoddle Street in 1865.

STAFFORD STREET 1852 or earlier. Lots were advertised for sale in November 1852. Possibly named after the county town of Staffordshire, England.

STANTON STREET Job Stanton was the Mayor of Collingwood in 1884–5 and laid the foundation stone of the Town Hall in July 1885. The street came into existence between this time and 1887 when the Town Hall was completed; a number of building blocks were auctioned in April 1888.

STUDLEY STREET 1852 or earlier. Lots for sale in November 1852. **John Hodgson**, who owned land in Collingwood, used the name Studley (from Studley Park in his native Yorkshire) for several of his properties. There is no evidence that he owned land in this subdivision, but his property on the Kew side of the river was well-known by this time.

THOMPSON STREET 1857 or earlier.

TRENERRY CRESCENT Edwin Trenerry bought the eighty-six-acre paddock between Alexandra Parade, Hoddle Street, Johnston Street and the river from the Dight family in 1878 for £21,000 and put it up for auction as 262 building allotments. See Abbot Street for more details.

TRURO STREET Part of Edwin Trenerry's 1878 subdivision of Dight's Paddock, this was named after the Cornish town of Truro, near the place where Edwin had grown up.

TURNER STREET James Hobson Turner was a city wool broker who had a house and several allotments in Collingwood. He was elected to Council in February 1867 and was a councillor for a total of fifteen years, including terms as mayor in 1869–70 and 1877--78. In the 1860s he took over a woolwashing establishment near Church Street. He agitated for the repeal of the Yarra anti-pollution legislation along with other owners of noxious industries along the Yarra. Residents who complained to Council about the smell of his tannery got nowhere and nor did the Central Board of Health. In 1874 he joined a partner and established the **Denton Hat Mill** in Nicholson Street (still standing, but much enlarged, on the corner of Mollison Street) conveniently close to his tannery. It was claimed to be the first steam-powered hat factory in Australia. Turner Street was part of the Dight's Paddock subdivision and the only street not named after a personal contact of Edwin Trenerry.

VALIANT STREET Part of John Orr's 1852 subdivision of 'The Township of Abbotsford'.

VARIAN STREET See Yarra Street.

VERE STREET See Collingwood.

VICTORIA CRESCENT 1855 or earlier. It could have been named in honour of Queen Victoria, who ruled England from 1837 to 1901, or the state of Victoria (which had been named to honour the Queen)

VICTORIA PARK An area of about ten acres, this land was acquired by the City of Collingwood from Edwin Trenerry in the late 1870s. It was soon eagerly sought by local sporting teams and eventually became the home of the Mighty Magpies (Collingwood Football Club) for many years. More recently the fences have been removed and artworks, sculptures and photographs dotted about the ground provide entertaining and informative insights into its history, and despite the departure of the AFL team, the Collingwood AFLW and VFL teams play the majority of their home games at the venue.

VICTORIA STREET This was originally called Simpson's Road after <u>**Mr James Simpson**</u>, a magistrate who constructed a footpath and road in 1843 to serve his own and some neighbouring properties. The Simpsons are described by Georgiana McCrae as living at *The Grange*, the property later known as *Yarra Grange*, which originally extended to Victoria Street, the section from Southampton Crescent being sold off in the late 1850s. Although it was named Victoria Street in the 1850s it continued to be also known as Simpson's Road until well into the twentieth century.

WALMER STREET 1857 or earlier. A punt once ferried passengers between Abbotsford and Kew at this spot. The footbridge which still exists was first constructed in 1890-91, with the primary purpose of transporting fresh water from Dights Falls to the Botanic Gardens. The source of the name has not been confirmed, but could be connected to Walmer, Kent, where Wellington as Lord Warden resided in Walmer Castle. (This is the origin of the name of the Victorian gold mining town, Walmer, near Maldon). As the section of road on the Abbotsford side is very short, it seems probable that the name originated on the Kew/Studley Park section of the street, and it could have been connected to Walmer House, residence of Mr Joseph Lush.

WILLIAM STREET 1855 or earlier. Part of Charles Nicholson's land, it was possibly named after his uncle William who brought him up.

YARRA STREET A reference to the nearby river. The wider section between Nicholson Street and Clarke Street was originally called Varian Street which was created in 1852 and was changed to Yarra Street around 1900, to become a continuance of the section of Yarra Street between Hoddle Street and Nicholson Street which had existed from 1857 or earlier.

YARRA BANK COURT A late twentieth century development overlooking the river.

YARRA FALLS LANE A non-existing street name! A right of way serves residential development on the site of the former Yarra Falls spinning mill, and this name was informally assigned by the landowners at the time of development in the early twenty-first century, but never formally named. Confusingly, the name appears on Google Maps.

ZETLAND STREET 1857 or earlier. Could this be Abbotsford's shortest street? It runs off Victoria Crescent opposite Mollison Street. This area was mainly occupied by woolwashing and fellmongering works making use of the river but Zetland Street once gave access to a house as well, occupied by wool merchants Elliott and <u>**William Murray**</u>, and angled so the front veranda faced the river. Nowadays the street functions as a driveway to the neighbouring factories, which once manufactured products but are now fashion factory outlets. Zetland is an archaic spelling of Shetland.

CLIFTON HILL

Clifton Hill was not included in the 1838-1839 government auctions described above. When the municipality of East Collingwood was proclaimed on 24 April 1855, it extended as far north as Reilly Street (now Alexandra Parade), but within a few months the East Collingwood Local Committee petitioned for East Collingwood to annexe the area to the north which was eventually to be named Clifton Hill but was at first referred to as north Collingwood. Proclaimed in September 1855, the additional area was mostly Crown land but there was already a bluestone quarry near the Merri creek and three bluestone houses occupied by Samuel Ramsden and the Brown brothers, who unsuccessfully opposed the annexation to East Collingwood. Why did the municipality want this additional area? There were three reasons: to extend Collingwood's north-south streets (Smith, Wellington and Hoddle) northward to tap the traffic and trade from areas such as Heidelberg, to gain access to the quarrying area for street-making materials, and to acquire Crown land space for erecting public buildings.

The eastern and western sections of Clifton Hill showed different patterns of development. In 1864 the Crown land west of Hoddle Street was surveyed by surveyor Clement Hodgkinson and plans were drawn up showing most of the streets now in existence subdivided into large blocks for sale. Over the ensuing years the land purchasers subdivided these purchases into building blocks, but the area remained fairly sparsely inhabited until the 1880s building boom. Earlier buildings included the Gold Street State School, which opened in April 1874, the first Wesleyan Methodist church on the corner of Wellington and Hodgkinson Streets (1874), St Andrew's church in Gold Street, 1871 (since demolished) and William Fox's house on the corner of Hodgkinson and Gold Streets.

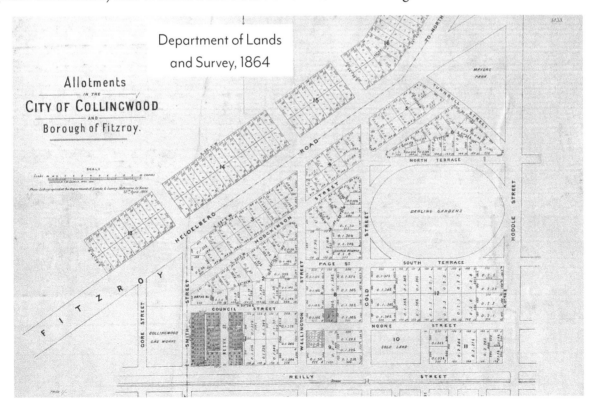

Department of Lands and Survey, 1864

On the eastern side the early settlers retained large landholdings, the quarries expanded, and noxious industries developed along Reilly Street (now Alexandra Parade east). A land sale in 1871 was the origin of the suburb's eventual name. Knipe and George's Property Exchange advertised in *The Argus* an auction to be held 18 Sep 1871 of allotments 'in future [to] be known as Clifton Hill'.

The origin of the name seems to be mired in speculation. According to Saxton, proprietor of a local newspaper *The Tribune*, **John Hanlon Knipe** chose the name as a reference to Clifton in England, but there are at least a dozen such place-names, none of which seem relevant to Knipe's origins, and Saxton provides no evidence. Another theory refers to a Clifton Farm as an early property in the district, but without any indication of its location. We do know that Clifton Grange, a handsome villa on about five acres, was located in Studley Park with a Yarra River frontage in the 1860s.

CLIFTON-HILL.—
That beautifully situated ground in the elevated position east of the Mayor's-park, and between Heidelberg-road and Ramsden-street, and will in future be known as

CLIFTON-HILL.
The ground has been surveyed, and all the streets are the Government width of 1 chain, and each allotment has a frontage to two streets. the lots varying in size, being suitable for cottages with gardens, and villas with extensive grounds.

The addition of 'Hill' to the name is easy – in the days of **miasma theory**, an elevated location was seen as more salubrious as well as providing good views.

In November 1872 Knipe held another auction of the remaining lots and the subdivision plan from this date has survived, so we know that it included Berry, Spensley, O'Grady, Fenwick, Grant and John Streets, with Rose, George and Lilly Streets as rear laneways. By this stage one villa had been built (on the corner of O'Grady and Berry Streets) and this was included in the auction. (See the next page for the plan).

This area was promoted as being not distant from the city, whereas areas of Clifton Hill further to the east had to wait some years before subdivision. But even Knipe's area was not extensively built on until later in the 1870s and 1880s.

Later subdivisions in the twentieth century include Ford Street, Brockenshire Street, Marshall Place and the development along Field Street, while in the twenty-first century new residential areas have been created in Park Place and the former Synthetics Dyeworks factory site off Noone Street.

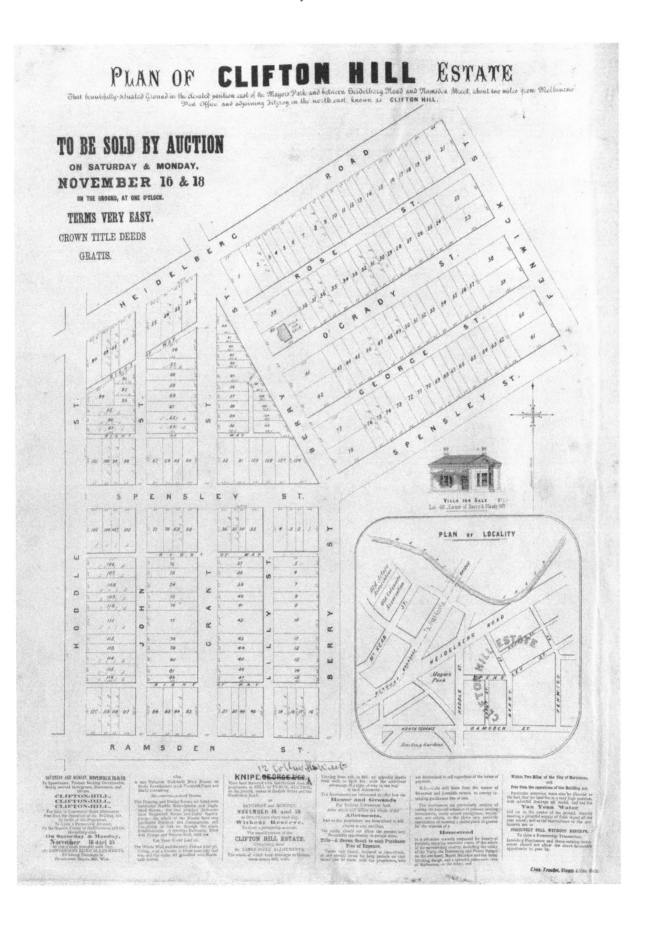

ABBOTT GROVE, CLIFTON HILL Dates from the mid 1880s. Probably named after Councillor Abbott.

A'BECKETT STREET The section of Noone Street from Hoddle Street to the Merri Creek was called a'Beckett Street on an early map and existed by 1857. Thomas a'Beckett, a solicitor who lived in Victoria Parade, was appointed council auditor in April 1856 and later in the same year was elected to Council and held the office of Mayor from 1856 to 1859.

AITKEN STREET Named in the late 1880s after Archibald Aitken, a councillor from 1881 to 1887 and Mayor in 1887, and named on the Town Hall foundation stone. He was the son of Thomas Aitken, who established the Victoria Brewery in 1854, began operating a distillery in Northumberland Street in 1862 and owned the freehold of several hotels. Aitken senior had also been a Councillor.

ALEXANDER STREET, CLIFTON HILL A later continuation of the street in Collingwood which had been named after one of the 1850s goldfields.

ANDERSON STREET Dates from the 1880s.

BARRIES PLACE One of three streets created in the residential development constructed on the site of the former Synthetic Dyeworks Industries Pty Ltd in Noone Street. Several names used in this development are non-conforming, because the current Guidelines do not support the use of first names. In 1958 Barrie Knight started the dyehouse which had previously housed a tannery.

BERRY STREET This may have been named after Graham Berry, who owned the *Collingwood Observer* in the early 1860s and represented Collingwood in the Legislative Assembly. It was one of the streets where lots were auctioned by John Hanlon Knipe in September 1871 and November 1872.

BROCKENSHIRE STREET This was a late subdivision in Clifton Hill, carried out by Edward Brockenshire, who lived at 107-109 Ramsden Street from around 1912 until his death in 1943 aged 78, and was a watchmaker and jeweller by trade. The street is lined with houses built at the same period and thus showing consistency in building style. The subdivision occurred in 1925–26. The Collingwood Council called for tenders for the construction of Brockenshire Street on 16 December 1925. In 1926 houses were being built and by 1928 eight houses had been constructed on the east side and six houses on the west side. 1A is a later addition, possibly on land excised from Mr Brockenshire's former house.

BROOKLYN TERRACE In recognition of a house formerly located at 1 Spensley Street named *Brooklyn*, this previously unnamed right of way behind 5 Spensley Street Clifton Hill and which runs between John Street and Grant Street, now provides vehicle access to the unit development that spans the block from John to Grant Streets. It was named in 2017.

CAROLINE STREET 1882 or earlier. Shown on plan of Waxman's Estate.

CLIFFORD PLACE Added during a late twentieth century housing development in Ramsden, Roseneath and Field Street.

CLIFTON AVENUE Samuel Ramsden had an extensive landholding between Ramsden Street and Roseneath Street; Clifton Avenue was created when the site was subdivided in 1888. It was first auctioned in October 1888 when Ramsden's house and a few blocks of land sold; John Vale & Son auctioned the remaining sites in December 1889.

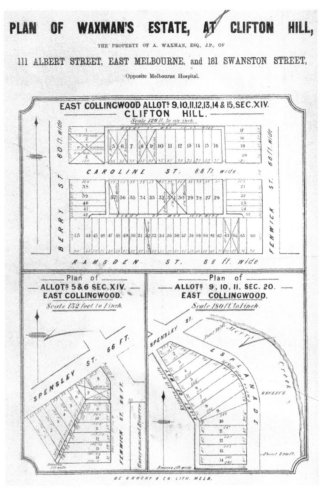

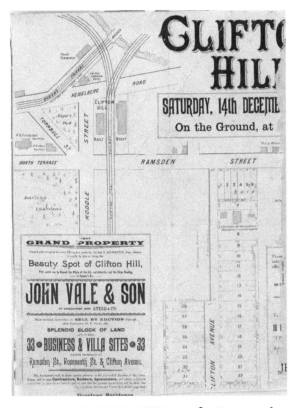

CLIFTON STREET 1870s, referring to the name of the suburb.

COPPER LANE The lane that runs beside the shot tower.

COULSON RESERVE This sports ground in Heidelberg Road was named in honour of E. Coulson, Mayor in 1907-08.

COUNCIL STREET Dating from the 1870s.

DALLY STREET The eastern portion of Dally Street is much earlier than the western end, which was not extended through to Clifton Avenue until many years after the 1888 subdivision of Samuel Ramsden's land. Thomas William Dally was a timber merchant in partnership with Thomas Luxford in Hoddle Street Abbotsford, and the two men owned land around Roseneath and Dally Streets which they auctioned in late 1889.

DARLING GARDENS This area was temporarily reserved as a site for public gardens in 1863 and proclaimed as such in 1878. Sir Charles Henry Darling was Governor of Victoria from 1863 to 1868. The gardens remain a place of leafy delight for local inhabitants and have been celebrated in the book *'I should be glad if a few more elms and oaks were included'*.

DUFFY STREET See O'Grady Street.

DUMMETT CRESCENT Harry Francis Dummett was a councillor throughout the 1950s and 1960s and mayor in 1956. This street was re-named when the overpass was constructed; before that it was simply part of Heidelberg Road.

DWYER STREET Dates from 1883. Named after Michael Dwyer, a justice of the peace and mayor from 1882 to 1884. A grocer and produce dealer, he served on council for eleven years.

EDMUND STREET Late 1880s.

THE ESPLANADE 1882 or earlier. See plan of Waxman's Estate at Caroline Street.

FENWICK STREET Early 1880s. Possibly connected to Orlando Fenwick, Mayor of Melbourne in the 1870s, after whom Fenwick Street Carlton is named, and who owned land in Collingwood.

FIELD/FEILD STREET 1880s. <u>William Guard Feild</u> was Collingwood's first Australian-born mayor in 1881–82, having first been elected to Council in 1879. The poor man was doomed to having the street named after him mis-spelt within a few years, but his name is correctly spelt on the Town Hall foundation stone.

FORD STREET Constructed in the 1920s when land subdivision took place, and named after owner, William Ford. The address of his house, now number 2, was originally Ramsden Street though the house was oriented with a view down the hill to the south.

GEORGE STREET 1871, designed as a rear right-of-way.

GORDON STREET 1890 approximately. Possibly named after Major-General Charles Gordon who had died at Khartoum in 1885.

GRANT STREET Mid 1870s.

GRAY STREET W. Gray was Mayor in 1885–56 and is honoured on the Town Hall foundation stone.

GROOM STREET Henry Groom of the Clifton Hill quarries was a big supplier of stone to the council and in common with a number of early Clifton Hill residents opposed the area's annexation to Collingwood in the 1850s. He unsuccessfully sought election to council in 1860 but was a Fitzroy councillor from 1858 to 1862.

HALL STREET Robert Hall was a woolwasher who set up in Reilly Street in 1871, having arrived from England in 1863. Despite protests from residents his business discharged its wastes into the Reilly

Street open drain. It became one of the most productive woolwashing works in Victoria and he was able to sell out for a big price in 1888. He was on council from 1890 to 1893. HALL RESERVE is on the Merri Creek side of The Esplanade.

HARRYS LANE A right of way within the early twenty-first century development of the former Dyeworks on the corner of Gray and Noone Streets. Harry and Grace lived on the southwest corner of Gray and Noone streets; 'Harry' (Paul Henry Bradley) had been a chimney sweep at the old Tannery and became the first employee at the dyeworks which was established on the site in 1958. A nonconforming street name according to current policy as first names are not supposed to be used.

HEIDELBERG ROAD The road to Heidelberg. See Queens Parade

HILTON STREET 1870s.

HILTON LANE

HODDLE STREET See Collingwood

HODGKINSON STREET Clement Hodgkinson was a surveyor in the Victorian Surveyor-General's office who prepared survey plans of Collingwood in 1853, 1856 and 1858, showing the progress of building development. He was appointed honorary consulting engineer to Collingwood Council in the 1850s. It is possible that he had some influence on the design of the Darling Gardens.

HORNE STREET Included on the 1905 MMBW Detail Plan but at that time the 1850s houses there still used Ramsden Street as their address. Other houses date from after 1911.

JOHN STREET A street in Knipe's 1871 subdivision.

KENT STREET 1870s.

KIEWA STREET 1884 or earlier. Probably named after Kiewa, a settlement in northwest Victoria.

KILGOUR CRESCENT The short section of Hoddle Street between Heidelberg Road and Queen's Parade used to be called Kilgour Crescent, as shown in Morgan's 1920 Street Directory. An Alexander Kilgour lived here in the 1880s. The street layout in this area was changed with the construction of the 1950s railway line overpass.

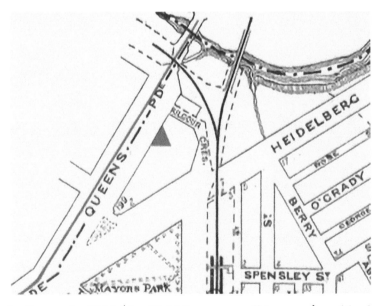

KNOTT'S RESERVE George Knott was a councillor in the 1960s and 1970s, including a term as Mayor. Knott competed in the London Olympic Games in 1948 (the 10,000-metre walking race) and had a long association with the Collingwood Harriers. He was also publican of the Yorkshire Stingo for many years.

LILLY STREET Shown on Knipe's 1872 subdivision plan.

LITTLE EDMUND STREET Connects Edmund Street and Clifton Street.

LITTLE WALKER LANE Originally a right of way, this now houses a number of residents

LOUISE STREET Added during a late twentieth century housing development in Ramsden, Roseneath and Field Street.

MARSHALL PLACE Three generations of the Marshall family were Collingwood councillors in the twentieth century. Walter Marshall was on council for 20 years, including a term as mayor in 1919–20; his son Laurie was mayor in 1936–37. Grandson Ttage (Nottage) was a councillor from the 1950s, serving the first of two terms as mayor in 1961 and finally retiring in 1980. The Marshall family also established a number of butcher shops in Clifton Hill and beyond. This street was developed on land which was the site of Sidchrome Industries from 1934 to 1959.

MAYOR'S PARK This park was included on the 1864 plan prepared by the Department of Lands and Survey. In 1870 the council minute book includes a petition from the inhabitants of North Fitzroy complaining of the depositing of night soil in the park.

MYRTLE STREET 1890

NOONE STREET John Noone was a lithographer in the Lands Department and served on council from 1860 to 1866 including two terms as mayor in 1861–2 and 1865–6. Noone lithographed a plan of west Clifton Hill in April 1864 showing Mayor's Park, Heidelberg Road, Council, Hodgkinson, Wellington, Gold, Page and Noone Streets and North and South Terrace. It was some years before many of these sites were settled.

NORTH TERRACE The poor condition of this street and its footpaths (located on the north side of the Darling Gardens) was mentioned in the council minute book on June 1st, 1870.

O'GRADY STREET The more westerly section between Berry and Fenwick Streets dates from Knipe's 1871 subdivision. The western and narrower section was first known as Duffy Street and dates from around 1876.

PAGE STREET James Page became the publican of the Galloway Arms Hotel in Johnston Street after starting out as a plumber. He was a councillor from 1863 until 1867, and again from 1870 until 1873. At the age of 84 he published his reminiscences in *The Observer* (the Collingwood and Fitzroy local paper) on 17 June 1909. Noone's 1864 map of west Clifton Hill shows Page Street. A number of building blocks owned by J Brown were auctioned in 1883.

PARK DRIVE A new subdivision in Clifton Hill dating from around 2000, its name referencing the surrounding parklands.

PARSLOW STREET Thomas Parslow owned land in the area bounded by Noone, Rutland, Hoddle and Roseneath Street, which was auctioned on 26 May 1883, described by the auctioneer as the Rutland Estate. This small street gave access to the building blocks of the subdivision and Parslow an opportunity for immortality. The balance was auctioned on 21 December 1887.

By October 1887 five houses in Parslow Street had been completed and another three were about to be built, but water had not been laid on; Council wrote to the Water Supply Department asking for a main to be laid in the street.

PECKVILLE STREET 1870s.

QUARRIES PARK This extensive park bordering Yambla Street and Ramsden Street was developed in the late twentieth century on land where bluestone had been quarried from the nineteenth century, and part of which was later used as the municipal tip.

QUEEN'S PARADE Originally known as Heidelberg Road, this road which started

CLIFTON HILL.
CITY OF COLLINGWOOD.
Hoddle, Rosneath, Noone, Parslow, & Rutland Sts.
TO CLOSE ACCOUNTS.

RUTLAND ESTATE

At Messrs. HAM'S ROOMS, Swanston Street,
WEDNESDAY, 21st DECEMBER, at 11 o'clock.

JOHN COVERLID In Conjunction with JOHN MILLS.

The Balance of the above Estate will be Sold by Auction, by order of the Executors of the late Geo. H. Knight and the representative of Thomas Parslow, Esq., who has left the Colony.

as the route from Melbourne to Heidelberg is one of Melbourne's oldest roads. It was later surveyed by Robert Hoddle and the wide road we see today was established at two chains in width (a little over 40 metres). Further along it divided and a separate road diverged northward. Called Plenty Road, it went to Northcote and the Plenty River area. In honour of Queen Victoria's golden jubilee, on 7 June 1887 the name change to Queens Parade was gazetted for the section of Heidelberg Road and Plenty Road from Northcote Bridge to Brunswick Street. On 10 August in the same year the Clifton Hill cable tram line from the city opened. Find out more here: **Queens Parade History Walk**

RAIN'S RESERVE William Rain was born in 1855 and lived in Collingwood from 1859 until 1916. An architect, he designed additions to Dr. Singleton's clinic in Wellington Street in 1890, and a number of local factories. From 1901 until 1916 he was a councillor and served one term as mayor in 1904–5. On 7 October 1907 Councillor Coulson moved that the small park at the intersection of Heidelberg Road and Queen's Parade be named in honour of Rain.

RAMSDEN STREET Samuel Ramsden worked the Clifton Hill Quarries and Ramsden Street started out as an access road to the quarries as well as the location of his bluestone house and those of his partners, which remain as the oldest houses in Clifton Hill. In April 1856 Ramsden, Henry Groom, and Henry and Charles Brown offered Council £200 if they would form and metal the then unnamed road. Within a year it was named; Ramsden was elected to council in 1857 and served for two years. RAMSDEN RESERVE, a sports oval, was developed in the twentieth century.

REEVES STREET Isaac Godfrey Reeves operated a wool washing establishment on the Yarra near Church Street and was elected to council in 1861, and was chairman in 1862. Later he was elected as a member of the Legislative Assembly for Collingwood and campaigned vigorously against the Yarra anti-pollution laws because of the threat they posed to the expansion of business in the Collingwood-Richmond area. He later suffered business failures and died in 1886. The street appears to have not been created until the early 1880s.

REILLYS WAY Part of a subdivision off Noone Street on the site of Synthetics Dyeworks Pty Ltd, a reference to the earlier name of Alexandra Parade.

ROSE STREET This was an anomaly in that it was named as a street but served as a back lane providing rear access to properties in neighbouring streets. In recent years, however, two structures at the rear of properties have been developed as residences. It appears to be one of the streets referred to by John Knipe in his 1871 advertisements as providing two street frontages for his building blocks.

ROSENEATH STREET 1855 or earlier. Possibly refers to Rosneath, Argyll and Bute, Scotland.

RUTLAND STREET 1881 or earlier. See also Parslow Street.

SMITH STREET See Collingwood.

SOUTH TERRACE Indicated on the 1864 Department of Lands and Survey map, on the south side of the Darling Gardens.

SPENSLEY STREET This was at first written as Spenceley and the western part of it dates from at least Knipe's 1871 auction sale. There were two men who might have had some connection with the naming of the street: James Spensley had an ironmongery on the corner of Brunswick and Moor Streets, Fitzroy from 1859 until 1871 and lived in Hoddle Street Collingwood from 1868 until 1871. Alternatively, a Howard Spenceley who arrived in Melbourne in 1858 lived in Gore Street Fitzroy in the 1860s before returning to England in 1872.

STAN STREET In 1959 Stan Fayman joined Barrie Knight as his business partner at Synthetics Dyeworks Pty Ltd.

TURNBULL STREET Henry Turnbull, a Scottish-born bootmaker, arrived in Sydney in 1838 where he became a noted participant in the anti-transportation agitation. He lived in Wellington Street, was active in the East Collingwood Local Committee from 1853-55, working for the establishment of local government, and was a councillor for most of the 1860s.

WALKER STREET Dates from at least 1885. Henry Walker was born in England in 1821 and arrived in Melbourne in 1855. In 1863 he became the owner of a soap and candle factory in Victoria Street on the Yarra where the Honeywell factory was later built (now Eden on the River). His business expanded and gave rise to many complaints from nearby residents including those in Kew about the 'unbearable odours'. In 1872 he was elected to Council and served altogether for twelve years, including five terms as mayor.

WELLINGTON STREET See Collingwood.

WILLIAM STREET Added during a new housing development in Ramsden, Roseneath and Field Street in the late twentieth century.

WRIGHT STREET 1885 or earlier. Andrew Wright was a councillor from 1874 until the 1880s. A property owner, he was described in *The Observer* as 'a rigid old Tory' who was opposed to tramways, municipal loans and 'such-like inventions of democracy'.

YAMBLA STREET 1884 or earlier. Probably named after the settlement of Yambla near Albury in NSW.

YARRABING LANE Named in March 2007. Yarrabing (which means the white gum) is the tree used by the Wurundjeri to welcome people to their lands. The Wurundjeri are the traditional custodians of the cultural heritage of this land.

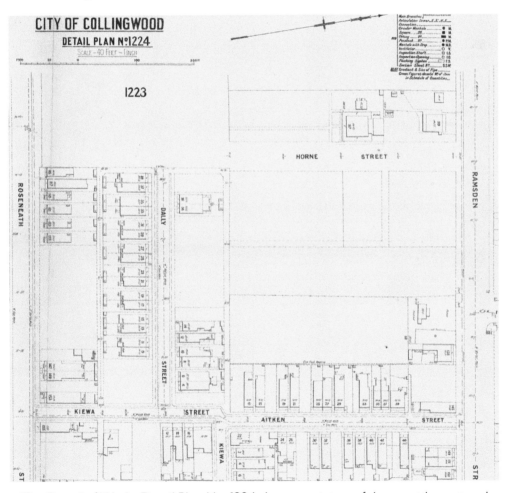

The Board of Works Detail Plan No. 1224 shows a mixture of dense settlement and vacant land in Clifton Hill in 1905

COLLINGWOOD

This area, closer to Melbourne, was densely settled quite early as many subdivisions began in the 1840s, not long after the original land purchases. Before long the 1850s gold rush gave a great impetus to the size of the population. Hodgkinson's 1858 map shows the pattern of settlement compared to the sparse buildings further from the centre of town.

ALEXANDER STREET, COLLINGWOOD Named after the Mt Alexander goldfield. The Collingwood section of this street was part of a small early 1850s subdivision with other streets also referring to goldfields. By the time of Hodgkinson's 1 January 1858 map some houses had been built here. Note Gold Street has not at this date been extended to the north or south.

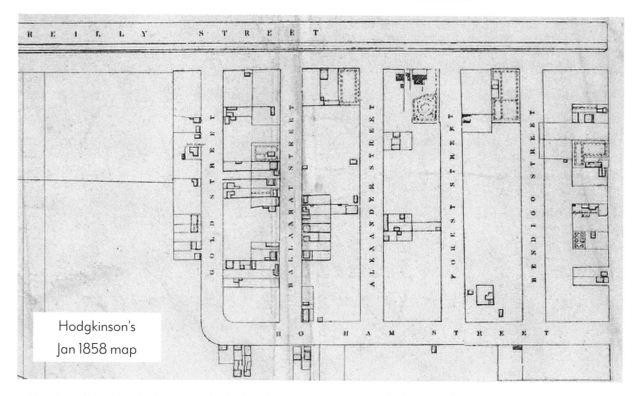

Hodgkinson's
Jan 1858 map

ALEXANDRA PARADE First called North Government Road, then Reilly Street, it was named after Francis Reilly, a Melbourne City Councillor, at a meeting of the Melbourne City Council in May 1851. The Fitzroy section was re-named in honour of Princess Alexandra of Denmark who married the Prince of Wales, later Edward VII. The Collingwood section continued to be called Reilly Street or Reilly Parade until 1908. The centre of the parade, now grassed over, was the site of a malodorous open drain from 1856. The section of the drain between Wellington and Smith Streets was not covered in until the 1920s.

BALLARAT STREET Early 1850s, named after the Gold Rush town.

BEDFORD STREET 1853 or earlier. Probably named after Bedford Street in London.

BENDIGO STREET Early 1850s, named after the Gold Rush town.

BLANCHE STREET Dates from the late 1860s. Named after a daughter of Charles Mater, landowner and owner of the Gasometer Hotel. See Mater Street for more details.

BREWERY LANE A newly named (2010s) thoroughfare within the Yorkshire Brewery development.

BROWN STREET Dating from 1854 or earlier, this street was named after Charles and Henry Brown who were early Clifton Hill landowners and developers.

BUDD STREET This street certainly existed in May 1856 when the residents complained to the Council that it was impassable! It originally ended at Easey Street. The section immediately south of Alexandra Parade was originally called Henry Street (q.v) and changed to Budd at the end of 1884.

BURLINGTON STREET, BURLINGTON TERRACE See Langridge Street.

BYRON STREET The existing Byron Street (off Northumberland Street) dates from the 1880s. The part of Park Street running off Victoria Street was originally called Byron Street and dates from 1857 or earlier.

CAMBRIDGE PLACE A short lane between Oxford Street and Cambridge Street.

CAMBRIDGE STREET 1852 or earlier. Named after the English university.

CAMBRIDGE STREET RESERVE a small park created in the twenty-first century from what was originally three building sites once inhabited by the Shakespeare family.

CAMPBELL STREET This might have been named after Daniel Stodhart Campbell, a Melbourne City councillor, in 1851. There were also two men named Campbell who owned large parcels of land in Collingwood, though not in this Portion, the pastoralist J.D.L. Campbell (one of the wealthiest men in Victoria) and an army officer, P.L. Campbell. The street was certainly in existence in 1853.

CHARLOTTE STREET 1860s. Named after Jane Charlotte Mater, wife of Charles Mater, landowner. See Mater Street for more detail.

CROMWELL STREET 1850 or earlier. Oliver Cromwell led armies of the Parliament of England against King Charles I, subsequently ruling as Lord Protector of the Commonwealth from 1653 until 1658 during England's period of republicanism. This undated subdivision plan of parts of Portions 53, 54 and 55 between Victoria Parade and Gipps Street shows a number of other streets whose names indicate links to the same period of English history: Prince Rupert was a Royalist cavalry commander during the Civil War, Rokeby is a poem about the Civil War.

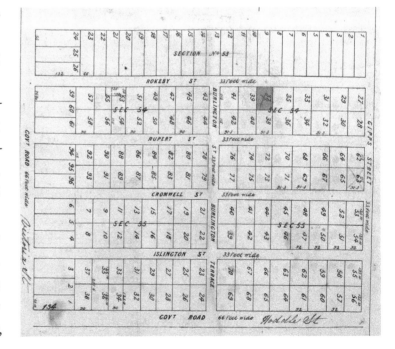

DERBY STREET 1840s. Edward Geoffrey Smith Stanley, the 14th Earl of Derby (1799-1869), was an English politician, Colonial Secretary in the 1830s and later Prime Minister. This street was part of an early Collingwood subdivision in 1840, called the Walmer Estate, sold by Charles Hutton who had bought Portions 52, 53 and 68 – 74 acres in all. The streets were named after 'men of note' according to Garryowen, and the initial subdivision consisted mainly of large allotments. Hutton was still subdividing and selling off allotments in the 1850s.

DIGHT STREET Part of R Henry Way's 1853 subdivision called Islington. While **Way** chose family names for several of the streets, this name may relate to the Dight family who operated Dight's flour mill near the junction of the Yarra River and the Merri Creek until the late 1850s.

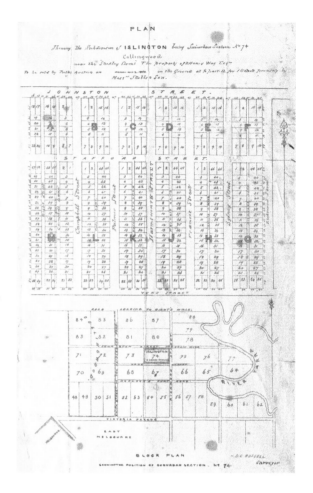

DORSET STREET 1857 or earlier. Probably named after the English county or the London street.

DOWN STREET 1857 or earlier.

EASEY STREET 1853 or earlier, named after an estate agent and auctioneer William Easey who managed the sale of the subdivisions of portions 80 and 81 in 1850.

ELIZABETH STREET See Langridge Street

EMERALD STREET 1857 or earlier.

EMMA STREET Dates from the late 1860s. Daughter of Charles Mater, landowner and owner of the Gasometer Hotel. See Mater Street for more detail.

FIFE STREET See Oxford Street

FOREST STREET 1855 or earlier. Named after a Victorian goldfield, along with Ballarat, Bendigo Streets.

FRANCIS STREET Part of the 1853 subdivision called the Islington Estate in Portion 74, owned by Sydney solicitor Richard Henry Way. Francis was one of his sons.

GIPPS STREET Sir George Gipps was Governor of N.S.W. from 1837 to 1846. The section between Hoddle Street and Wellington was originally a separate street called Hodgson's Road, named after John Hodgson, a merchant who was one of the district's early landowners, having purchased four Crown portions which he subdivided over the 1840s and 1850s. He also owned the Studley Arms Hotel in Wellington Street (now demolished). Council minute books from 1856 onwards report numerous discussions relating to re-aligning and widening the street to make one through road.

This involved Council in buying seventeen properties, including eight houses. Before this a drain ran along Gipps Street, crossed at intervals by wooden bridges. In 1867 this was replaced by underground brick drains, said to be the first of their kind in Australia.

GLASGOW STREET 1853 or earlier. Presumably named after the city in Scotland.

GLASSHOUSE LANE This was off 118 Wellington Street, providing on its south side rear access to Glasshouse Road properties, but with a number of houses on the north side. It no longer exists.

GLASSHOUSE ROAD Victoria's first glass factory (and one of only two factories in Collingwood until 1851) was in Rokeby Street. The build-

Glasgow and Silver Streets depicted ca 1935 by the Housing Investigation and Slum Abolition Board

ing continued to be known as the Glasshouse although by 1856 it had become a candle factory.

GOLD STREET The section south of Alexandra Parade was subdivided by speculators in 1850-52 but remained largely useless until after underground drainage was installed in 1867. The street's name relates to the precious metal foremost in everybody's minds during the gold rush.

HARMSWORTH STREET This street was included on an 1853 subdivision plan of the Islington Estate, owned by Richard Henry Way, a Sydney solicitor. Harmsworth was his mother's maiden name and the name given to one of his sons.

HENRY STREET Part of Charles Mater's subdivision dating from the 1860s and named after his son. This short street ran from Reilly Street (Alexandra Parade) to Mater Street, to the east of Blanche Street, and by the 1880s became the continuation of Budd Street.

HODDLE STREET Born in London in 1794, Robert Hoddle was appointed assistant surveyor in Sydney in 1823 and eventually became deputy surveyor- general. The work for which he is chiefly remembered is the laying out of Melbourne in 1837, when he acted as auctioneer at the first land sale. When, in 1851, Victoria became independent of New South Wales, Hoddle was made the new state's first Surveyor-General.

HODGSON'S ROAD or Hodgson's Punt Road See Gipps Street.

HOOD STREET Thomas Hood was born in Scotland in 1826 and arrived in Australia in 1849. After spending some time on the goldfields, he opened Collingwood's first bakery in 1852 on the corner of Wellington and Stanley Streets. He later began a maltster's business. He was active in having Collingwood proclaimed a municipality and was one of the assessors at the first election in conjunction with John Pascoe Fawkner. He was the rate collector for 27 years and was a councillor from 1857 to 1860 and again in 1887. Hood Street was left facing Hoddle Street when the road widening in the 1970s resulted in the demolition of a whole block of buildings on the west side of Hoddle Street.

HOTHAM STREET Early 1850s (see Ballarat and Bendigo Streets) between Hoddle and Gold Street. It was probably named after Sir Charles Hotham who succeeded La Trobe as Governor of Victoria in 1853. The section that runs east from Smith Street was originally a separate street called Simson Street that ended at Charlotte Street, and was re-named Hotham Street in November 1884.

ISLINGTON STREET 1853. Probably named after the district of Islington in London.

JAMES STREET Called St. James Street on Hodgkinson's 1858 map and council's 1850s list of streets.

JOHN STREET Now functioning mainly as rear access, there were once houses sited on the east side, running north-south from Little Smith Street (now Singleton Street) to Vere Street.

JOHNSTON STREET Named in 1851 after Alderman J. S. Johnston of the Melbourne City Council. Previously referred to as Government road.

KEELE STREET This street was originally called Ryrie Street but was changed in honour of William Keele who was mayor in 1889–90, having earlier served as a councillor in the late 1870s. James Stewart Ryrie was an early landowner and the area bounded by Ryrie, Reilly, Gold and Smith Streets (Portion 86) was referred to as Ryrie's Paddock in the 1850s. Houses existed here from as early as 1852, but further building lots, between Budd and Hoddle Streets, were auctioned as advertised in *The Argus*, 4 July 1860, page 2 and the subdivision plan shown below was provided for prospective purchasers.

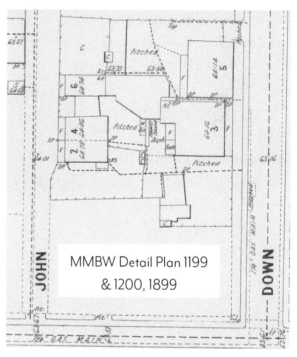

MMBW Detail Plan 1199 & 1200, 1899

Sales by Auction.

THIS DAY.
At Twelve o'clock Sharp.
Valuable Building Allotments, having Frontages to Hoddle and Great Ryrie streets, Collingwood.
To Tradesmen, Speculators, Builders, and Others.

Greig and Murray have received instructions from the mortgagee, to sell by auction, at their rooms, on Wednesday, 4th inst., at twelve o'clock,
All those valuable building allotments, being numbered in the plan of subdivision as lots 22, 23, 26 of section 80, of the parish of Jika Jika, county of Bourke.
Lots 22 and 23, having a frontage of 66 feet to Great Ryrie street, by a depth of 66 feet more or less.
Lot 26, having a frontage of 25 feet to Hoddle street, by a depth of 67 feet more or less.

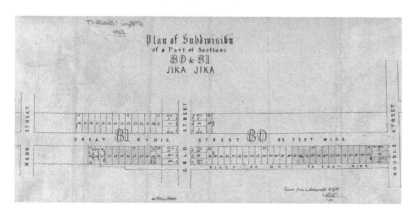

LANG STREET John Lang was born in Scotland and arrived in Australia in 1858. A tailor and outfitter and a director of the Langridge Building Society, he was elected to Council in 1881 and served for 6 years. He later became a Justice of the Peace and served as Collingwood's Librarian from 1905 to 1919 when he retired at the age of 83.

LANGRIDGE STREET George David Langridge was born in 1829 in Kent and arrived in Australia in 1852 as a carpenter. He worked initially as a general contractor then as an estate agent and later as an architect. In 1883 he built himself a mansion at 12 North Terrace with a commanding view of the Darling Gardens. He was a councillor from 1865 until 1873, with two terms as mayor. He entered parliament in 1874 and died in 1891. The street had its origins in two short and narrow streets: Elizabeth Street which ran from Wellington Street to Rokeby Street and was described by residents in the 1850s as muddy and almost impassable in winter, and Burlington Street (after Burlington Arcade in London?) connecting Rokeby and Hoddle Streets. A number of businessmen (some of them councillors) agitated for the improvement of the street as part of a plan to enhance their business prospects with a wide thoroughfare connecting busy Gertrude Street and the Studley Park Bridge. The final form of the street, although still necessitating considerable expenditure in acquiring property, was a rather reduced version of this grandiose vision. The section between Smith Street and Little Oxford Street was formed and built on in 1872 but not proclaimed for a number of years, probably because of Council's policy of not proclaiming streets public until property owners had properly constructed them. The connection between Little Oxford and Wellington Streets was not made until 1882. Look down this street and you will see that it still does not run in a straight line.

LITTLE .... There are many streets in Collingwood starting with the word "Little" and running parallel with the street of the same name. In many cases these simply function as lanes but there are some exceptions, and these are described below.

LITTLE BEDFORD STREET Off 248 Wellington Street, this ran through to Emerald Street but disappeared with the construction of Housing Commission flats. Peter Petherick who owned the Studley Arms Hotel on the corner with Wellington Street was in trouble with council in 1869 and 1870 for erecting a fence across the street. There was dispute about whether John Hodgson had owned the land, but in April 1870 council declared it a public thoroughfare.

LITTLE HARMSWORTH STREET Marked on the 1853 plan of the Islington Estate as Harmsworth Lane.

LITTLE OXFORD STREET This is a proper street dating from the same time as Oxford Street.

LITTLE SMITH STREET Now Singleton Street (q.v). This was a real exception to the usual pattern in being located at some distance from Smith Street! While narrow, it was a street in its own right, dates from at least 1857, and was once occupied by several houses.

LITTLE WELLINGTON STREET This runs off Wellington Street rather than parallel to it and is a proper street, which housed a number of residents in the nineteenth century.

MCNAMARA RESERVE A fairly recent playground pocket park on the corner of Gold Street and Keele Street.

MANSARD LANE Early twenty-first century addition following the re-development of the former Yorkshire Brewery into residences. A reference to the roof design of the brew tower.

MASON STREET 1856 or earlier. There was a councillor James Mason (a baker in Wellington Street) from 1858 until 1860 but it is not known whether he had any connection with the street. A John Mason owned a number of properties in Mason Street and Victoria Parade.

MATER STREET In the 1850s Charles Mater owned the land in Portion 86, originally Ryrie's Paddock, in the area which now includes Mater Street and neighbours the Gasometer Hotel which Mater also owned by 1864. The area was poorly drained and in 1856 Mater attended council meetings with consulting engineer Clement Hodgkinson regarding drainage proposals. It was not subdivided until the late 1860s when, as well as Mater, streets were named Blanche and Emma after his daughters, Henry after his son, and Charlotte and Simson after his wife. Lots were promoted as providing an opportunity for the working man to acquire home ownership. Mater, comfortably off, returned to his native Germany with his family, leaving disgruntled ratepayers to negotiate for years with council over the state of their roads and drains, petitioning council in 1873, holding public meetings in 1873 and 1876, and offering to pay half the costs of road forming and channelling.

In October 1875 the Health Officer visited Mater's paddock and found the channels full of sewage and choked up with offensive matter. Once water was laid on matters became even worse; as water no longer needed to be carted people used more, so there was a greater flow of water in the channels which with no means of escape became stagnant. In wet weather children could not go to school. A letter to *The Mercury* claimed that the streets 'are at the present time a standing disgrace to the town of Collingwood, an eyesore to the neighbourhood, and the sure means of destroying the health of its inhabitants'.

Council continued to insist all streets must be properly constructed by the owners before they could be proclaimed public streets or taken under the management of the council.

MCCUTCHEON WAY Andrew McCutcheon started his political career as a Collingwood councillor in the 1960s and was mayor in 1975–76. He was later Attorney-General and the Minister for Planning and Housing. This is the most recent example of a street named after a councillor.

MONTAGUE STREET On 1858 map and 1857 list. A London street, but given its proximity to streets named with an English Civil War theme could be a mis-spelling of Edward Montagu who was a loyal supporter of Oliver Cromwell.

MONTALTO LANE Named in December 2018 in recognition of Joe Montalto. The property that abuts the entire eastern boundary of the lane was purchased by Joe and John Montalto in the early 1960s. Joe and John built and ran a service station and mechanical repair workshop from the site until 2003. Following the closure of the service station, Joe's children developed the property into an apartment building, and many of them still own properties within the residential block. There are now grandchildren of Joe Montalto living on the site.

NAPOLEON STREET 1851 or earlier. Part of Portion 73 subdivision. Napoleon I (1769-1821) was Emperor of France from 1804-14 and again in 1815. Given Napoleon's defeat by Wellington, it may have been someone's idea of a joke to name this insignificant street, running off what was at that time the important and populous Wellington Street, after the Emperor.

NORTHUMBERLAND STREET 1851 or earlier. Named after the English county, the London avenue, or the 10th Earl of Northumberland who wavered between supporting Charles I and the Parliamentarians.

OTTER STREET 1852 or earlier. The Reverend George Otter was a Launceston resident who bought 26 acres of Crown Land in 1839 Portion 73 and subdivided the area south of Johnston Street and east of Smith Street in the late 1840s.

OXFORD PLACE A lane off Oxford Street.

OXFORD STREET 1852 or earlier. Named after the English university town in company with Cambridge Street, to which it runs parallel. The section between Mason Street and Derby Street was originally called Fife Street.

OXFORD STREET PARK The City of Yarra has a policy of adding to open space. This recent pocket park was created in 2012-2013 by closing off a short section of Oxford Street between Langridge Street and Derby Street and was designed by **Urban Initiatives**.

PALMER STREET Shown on the 1853 subdivision plan of the Islington Estate and possibly named after Sir James Palmer, an English doctor who was mayor of Melbourne in 1845-46 and later a member of Parliament.

PARADE PLACE A short dead-end street, accommodating four houses off Victoria Parade in the nineteenth century, which no longer exists. In the 1930s the Housing Investigation and Slum Abolition Board found three double-fronted brick houses, all damp and condemned but tenanted.

Parade Place ca 1935

PEEL STREET Garryowen in his *Chronicles of Early Melbourne* describes this area as the first subdivision of the Walmer Estate, sold by Charles Hutton, with streets named after 'men of note' The subdivision took place on February 15th, 1840, and the man of note in this case was presumably Sir Robert Peel, the English politician who became Home Secretary in 1822. His term of office was made famous by the creation of the Metropolitan Police Force, whose members were nicknamed after him 'peelers' or 'bobbies'. He was Prime Minister from 1841 to 1846.

PEEL STREET PARK Collingwood became a little greener with the opening of this park in 2011. The site had been a car park for some years but until the 1950s was occupied by the very imposing Oxford Street Congregational Church, whose hall still stands to the west of the park.

PERRY STREET 1849-1851 or earlier. Part of the Rev George Otter's subdivision. A contractor called Eli Perry lived in the area, having arrived in Australia in 1849, but there is no direct evidence that the street name relates to him. A number of auctions in the 1850s were carried out by "Symons and Perry" and this is perhaps the more likely connection.

PRINCES STREET 1855 or earlier. A London street.

RAPHAEL STREET On the 1857 list of East Collingwood streets.

REILLY STREET See Alexandra Parade.

RICHMOND LANE 1853. This right-of-way serving Sydney Street became an adjunct to the footpath when Hoddle Street was widened in the early 1970s.

ROBERT STREET 1855 or earlier.

ROKEBY STREET 1850 or earlier. *Rokeby* is the title of a poem by Sir Walter Scott with an English Civil War theme set in Rokeby Park and first published in 1813. See Cromwell Street for a subdivision plan.

Rokeby St in the 1930s

RUPERT STREET 1850 or earlier. It was perhaps named after Prince Rupert, a Royalist cavalry commander during the Civil War. In May 1856 council received a petition from thirty-one owners and occupiers complaining of the poor condition of the street due to alterations to streets on a higher level which caused drainage problems.

RUSSELL STREET 1850s. Residents complained to Council about the state of its footpath in 1873. Perhaps named after the London street.

RYRIE STREET See Keele Street.

SACKVILLE STREET 1851 or earlier. A London street.

SCOTT STREET Listed on the 1857 *East Collingwood Streets*, but not located.

SILVER STREET 1857 or earlier.

SIMSON STREET See Hotham Street. This was part of Charles Mater's subdivision and ran from Smith Street to Charlotte Street. Simson was the prior married surname of Mater's wife Jane Charlotte.

SINGLETON STREET This 1850s street was originally called Little Smith Street, but an alternative was sought around the early twentieth-first century because of confusion with the street of the same name in Fitzroy. Dr John Singleton was a medical doctor and benefactor of the poor of the district. The striking building still located on the southeast corner of Wellington Street and Singleton Street opened in January 1889 as his medical dispensary.

SMITH STREET This was one of the streets proclaimed and named at the meeting of the Melbourne City Council on May 23rd, 1851. John Thomas Smith was a Melbourne City alderman who was seven times elected mayor. The street had formerly been referred to as the Eastern Road or the Heidelberg Road.

STANLEY STREET Stanley was the family name of the Earls of Derby. (See also the information under Derby Street). An alternative suggestion is that it was named after the captain of the H.M.S. Rattlesnake on which Governor Bourke came to Port Phillip in 1836. This street was part of Captain Hutton's 1840 subdivision. Building lots were also for sale in 1851.

STURT STREET Although located in an area which was subdivided by the 1850s, this street may not have been created until the 1880s.

SYDNEY STREET One of the streets in the 1853 subdivision called the Islington estate, owned by Sydney solicitor Richard Henry Way. Sydney was one of his sons.

TAVARES LANE A previously unnamed right of way between Perry Street and Johnston Street, named in 2018 in recognition of Antonio Tavares 1944-2017. Tavares was an active member of the Collingwood community and operated a boxing gym in the basement of the Collingwood Housing Estate in Hoddle Street (also his residence) from 2000 until at least 2008. He made a tangible contribution to disadvantaged residents.

VERE STREET 1853 or earlier. A London street.

VICTORIA PARADE This street existed under this name, honouring the Queen, from at least 1841, but was not officially proclaimed by Melbourne City Council until 1851.

WATERLOO ROAD 1856 or earlier. Waterloo was the site of Napoleon's defeat at the hands of the English military headed by the Duke of Wellington.

Waterloo Road depicted ca 1935 by the
Housing Investigation and Slum Abolition Board

Wellington Street in 1862, a busy local shopping street

WELLINGTON STREET This street was the major axis of a subdivision carried out in 1849 by <u>Captain Charles Hutton</u> and finishing at Johnston Street. In the 1850s it was Collingwood's most densely populated and busy street with many shops and businesses. By 1869 council had formed a Wellington Street Extension Committee to work on acquiring private properties to allow for its extension northwards. In 1871 the section from Johnston Street to Reilly Street (now Alexandra Parade) was formed and metalled. The Duke of Wellington was famous for his defeat of Napoleon at Waterloo in 1815. Nicknamed the 'Iron Duke' he was Prime Minister of England from 1828 to 1830 and again in 1834.

YORK STREET 1857 or earlier. Probably named after the English city, the London street or the Duke of York.

SOURCES AND FURTHER READING

Books

Australian Dictionary of Biography. Melbourne: M.U.P., 1966 – 2012.

Barrett, Bernard *The Inner Suburbs: the evolution of an industrial area*. M.U.P. 1971.

Barrett, Bernard 'The Making of an Industrial Environment.' Collingwood, Victoria, 1851-91 (A thesis submitted for the degree of Master of Arts in the Department of History). University of Melbourne, 1970.

Cummings, Karen *Streets of Collingwood* Abbotsford, Collingwood Historical Society, 1991.

Garryowen *The Chronicles of Early Melbourne, 1835 to 1852*. Melbourne: Fergusson and Mitchell, 1888.

Georgiana's Journal: Melbourne 1841-1865. Edited by Hugh McCrae. 2nd ed. Angus and Robertson, 1966.

Hibbins, G.M., *A short history of Collingwood*, Abbotsford, Collingwood Historical Society, 1997.

Meyer, Tina, *"I should be glad if a few elms and oaks were included": the Darling Gardens Clifton Hill*, Abbotsford, Collingwood Historical Society, 1995.

Saxton, John George, *Victoria place-names and their origin*, Clifton Hill, Saxton and Buckie, 1907.

Sutherland, Alexander *Victoria and its Metropolis*. Melbourne: McCarron Bird, 1888.

Directories

Sands and Kenny's Melbourne Directory 1857-1861.

Sands and McDougall's Melbourne Directory 1862-1919.

Victorian Municipal Directory (various years).

Melbourne Street Directory (Morgan) 1920

Council Documents

Collingwood Council Rate Books, 1864 to 1930

Collingwood Council Minute Books, 1855-1876.

Collingwood Council Outward Letter Books (VPRS 11141/P1 Unit 10-14)

Collingwood Council Finance and Rate Committees Minute Book (VPRS 11087/P3)

Newspapers

The Age, The Argus, The Herald, The Melbourne Daily News and Port Phillip Patriot, Port Phillip Gazette

Yarra News August-September 2019, page 5

Trove Newspapers list: 'Streets of Collingwood' **https://trove.nla.gov.au/list/41035**

Maps and Plans

Map of Melbourne and suburbs (James Kearney). 1855.

Map of Collingwood (Proeschel). 1855?

Plan of the Streets and Buildings in East Collingwood (Clement Hodgkinson). Jan 1st, 1858.

Allotments in the City of Collingwood and Borough of Fitzroy, Melbourne: Dept. of Lands & Survey, 1864: http://search.slv.vic.gov.au/permalink/f/1tla8hv/SLV_VOYAGER2135611

Plan of Melbourne and its Suburbs (H. Byron Moore, Assistant Surveyor General). September 1879.

Map of the City of Collingwood (C. Woodhouse). 1885.

https://collingwoodhs.org.au/wp-content/uploads/2015/09/File-490.pdf

Melbourne and Metropolitan Board of Works maps and detail plans 1897 to 1905

Municipality of Collingwood. 1931.

Subdivision Plans

The Campbellfield Estate:
   http://search.slv.vic.gov.au/permalink/f/1o9hq1f/SLV_VOYAGER2150099

The township of Abbotsford:
   http://search.slv.vic.gov.au/permalink/f/1o9hq1f/SLV_VOYAGER2172150

Plan of subdivision of portion of Section 56, Byron, Allan, Henry, Raphael Street etc:
   http://handle.slv.vic.gov.au/10381/161583

Fairchild Estate:
   http://search.slv.vic.gov.au/permalink/f/1o9hq1f/SLV_VOYAGER2115432

Charles Nicholson property:
   http://handle.slv.vic.gov.au/10381/262160

Cromwell Street etc subdivision plan:
   http://handle.slv.vic.gov.au/10381/160125

Plan of subdivision of the Grosvenor Estate:
   http://search.slv.vic.gov.au/permalink/f/1o9hq1f/SLV_VOYAGER2547974

Plan of allotments in west Clifton Hill:
   http://search.slv.vic.gov.au/permalink/f/1tla8hv/SLV_VOYAGER1825916

Plan of Clifton Hill Estate:
   http://search.slv.vic.gov.au/permalink/f/1o9hq1f/SLV_VOYAGER2547744

Clifton Avenue, Steed and Smith auction plan:
   http://search.slv.vic.gov.au/permalink/f/1tla8hv/SLV_VOYAGER1171288

Clifton Avenue, John Vale auction plan:

http://search.slv.vic.gov.au/permalink/f/1tla8hv/SLV_VOYAGER1173217

Waxman's Estate:

http://search.slv.vic.gov.au/permalink/f/1tla8hv/SLV_VOYAGER1620420

Rutland Estate:

Great Ryrie Street 1859:

http://search.slv.vic.gov.au/permalink/f/1o9hq1f/SLV_VOYAGER2165872

Aitken, Kiewa and Ramsden St subdivision:

http://search.slv.vic.gov.au/permalink/f/1tla8hv/SLV_VOYAGER1173215

Grosvenor Estate:

http://search.slv.vic.gov.au/permalink/f/1o9hq1f/SLV_VOYAGER2547974

Ryrie Budd Streets 1869:

http://search.slv.vic.gov.au/permalink/f/1o9hq1f/SLV_VOYAGER2039677

Vale and Company collection of real estate plans, State Library of Victoria.

Biographical Material

http://adb.anu.edu.au/biography/clarke-sir-andrew-3219

https://adb.anu.edu.au/biography/knipe-john-hanlon-3967

https://collingwoodhs.org.au/resources/notable-people-2/

https://www.parliament.vic.gov.au/about/people-in-parliament/re-member/details/24/796

Photos and Paintings

Blind Creek 1854:

https://victoriancollections.net.au/items/5e2ccabd21ea671428127ece

Foy and Gibson emporium and factories:

https://www.picturevictoria.vic.gov.au/site/yarra_melbourne/Collingwood/21120.html

Johnston Street postcard:

http://handle.slv.vic.gov.au/10381/101158

Parade Place:

http://handle.slv.vic.gov.au/10381/270533

River Terrace in flood:

http://search.slv.vic.gov.au/permalink/f/cjahgv/SLV_VOYAGER1741370

Rokeby St:

http://handle.slv.vic.gov.au/10381/270564

Smith Street postcards ca 1906 to ca 1908:

> http://handle.slv.vic.gov.au/10381/289461
> http://handle.slv.vic.gov.au/10381/289289
> http://handle.slv.vic.gov.au/10381/251816
> http://handle.slv.vic.gov.au/10381/289431

Waterloo Road ca 1935:

> http://handle.slv.vic.gov.au/10381/270599

Wellington Street 1862:

> http://handle.slv.vic.gov.au/10381/290069

You can find other photographs on the following sites:

Collingwood Historical Society Flickr account and Streets album:

> https://www.flickr.com/people/collingwoodhs/
> https://www.flickr.com/photos/collingwoodhs/albums/72157632349638135

Picture Victoria:

> https://picturevictoria.vic.gov.au

State Library of Victoria:

> https://www.slv.vic.gov.au (select 'pictures & photographs' or 'maps')

Royal Historical Society of Victoria:

> http://collections.historyvictoria.org.au/rhsvdatabases/imagesonline.htm

Trove images:

> https://trove.nla.gov.au/search/advanced/category/images